I0465086

I. Introduction

Resale price maintenance (RPM) continues to be a contentious topic, both in economics and in antitrust. During the 1980s economists derived new efficiency motivations for RPM while the Supreme Court reaffirmed the decades-old *per se* ban on its use and Congress threatened to extend that ban. In the 1990s, after several years of federal inactivity during the Reagan Administration, the Federal Trade Commission (FTC) has once again begun bringing RPM cases.[1]

While economists have proposed a number of different efficiency explanations for RPM, such theorizing has been performed largely without the help of businesses that actually use RPM. With little practical evidence, such hypotheses have been subject to substantial criticism. Of course, since RPM has been *per se* illegal, businesses may be reluctant to admit that they are engaged in the practice, which would appear to be a necessary condition for generating an efficiency defense. This paper seeks to find out why businesses may believe that they benefit from RPM. It does so by examining which efficiency rationales were advanced by firms during a critical time for RPM in the United States, 1915 to 1917. These rationales, drawn largely from previously unexplored materials, are then examined in the light of current economic theory. There are two basic sources for these rationales. The first is three hearings on RPM held in 1915, 1916, and 1917 in the U.S. House of Representatives on a bill to legalize certain forms of RPM. The second is the transcript of seven days of hearings the FTC held in 1917 to discuss efficiency motivations for RPM.

Section II explains several economic theories that have been posited for RPM and briefly discusses the critiques of these theories that have arisen in the legal and economic communities. Section III examines federal RPM case law prior to 1918 and posits efficiency rationales from Section II to match the products involved in the case law. Section III also discusses the uncertainty in the case law during the period 1908 to 1917 and the concepts behind the various judicial

---

[1] See Kreepy Krauly, USA, 56 Federal Register 1813, January 17, 1991, and Nintendo of America, Inc., 56 Federal Register 15883, April 18, 1991. Prior to these cases, the last RPM case brought by the FTC was Germaine Monteil Cosmetiques Corp., 100 F.T.C. 543 (1982).

decisions. Section IV presents the efficiency arguments made during this period of legal uncertainty for RPM. Section IV also shows that RPM had support from diverse sources, including Thomas Edison, Louis Brandeis, and apparently Henry Ford, as well as the president of the National Housewives League and the Consulting Home Editor of the *Ladies' Home Journal.*

The hearings, despite being held over 70 years ago, disclose the same motivations for RPM that scholars use today. These motivations were presented largely without the assistance of economists. Yet in many circumstances the efficiency arguments were presented, while not with technical rigor, accurately and in a manner consistent with the current economic learning.

II. The Efficiency Theories for RPM - And Their Critics

Several efficiency rationales for RPM and other vertical restraints have emerged in the last thirty years in the economic literature. They compose a wide variety of efficiencies for a large number of goods.[2]

A. Horizontal Externalities: Special Services, Shelf Space and Information

The oldest efficiency story in the economic literature, presented by Telser (1960), may be put in the following way. A manufacturer places a new product, like a videocassette recorder (VCR), on the market. Before many or most sales take place, consumers have to be educated in how to use this product. If retailers incur costs teaching consumers how to work the VCR, the retailer must be compensated for its expenses by higher margins on its sales. Unfortunately for both manufacturers and full-service retailers, a customer may be able to take that training and go across the street and buy the VCR from a discount dealer who does not offer these services and thus does not incur the relevant costs, eliminating the retailer's incentive to provide such information. Without the protection of RPM or another similar instrument, manufacturers cannot

---

[2] The economics literature is not very clear on which vertical restraints are most efficient in particular circumstances. In the time period of this study, however, non-price vertical restraints such as exclusive dealerships and exclusive territories may have been rare because of the lack of chain stores and high transportation costs. This paper will not review all of the efficiency theories for the use of RPM and other vertical restraints. See Ippolito (1988 at 59-73, 1991 at 282-291) for a more extensive discussion and literature review.

prevent the existence of a "horizontal externality", with one retailer gaining benefit from the actions of another. Retailers will thus be reluctant to invest in educating customers, and therefore insufficient product information will be supplied to consumers.

The horizontal free-riding[3] argument, however, is not confined solely to complex goods. For instance, in the model of Marvel and McCafferty (1984), some retailers are assumed to have gained consumers' confidence. Consumers view these retailers as their agents in "certifying" which goods are of high quality. RPM-induced margins are thus the manufacturer's payments to the retailer for the costly quality certification of that retailers' goods. This certification is expected to be especially important for manufacturers who are attempting to create a brand name reputation for their own products, and for goods that have uncertain quality.

In addition, as Goldberg (1984) and Bittlingmayer (1988) point out, retailers' costly conveyance of information can take other forms. For instance, a manufacturer may want to buy high profile shelf space as a form of advertising. The RPM-induced higher margins through RPM, in effect, buy the more expensive shelf-space. Without RPM, consumers could gain this information at a high-priced store and use it to buy goods at a discount house.

One issue that has consistently arisen in the RPM debate is the desire of manufacturers to prevent their goods from being used as "loss leaders."[4] The only direct reference to this in the current economic literature, however, is a brief discussion by Marvel and McCafferty (1985 at 375). Marvel and McCafferty suggest that the desire to free-ride on shelf space explains this phenomena. They further argue that goods will be used as loss leaders when "the value of a well-known product line to a new entrant store is greater than to an established retail firm." In other words, manufacturers will use RPM to deter new entrant retailers from using their products as loss-leaders in order to "free-ride" off the shelf-space of established retailers.

---

[3] As Breit (1991 at 86) notes, one can consider the consumer rather than the discount dealer to be the free-rider.

[4] See, for example, Seligman and Love (1932 at 143-161). In Canada, the desire to avoid loss-leading is an exception to the per se rule against RPM. See Restrictive Trade Practises Commission (1955) and R. v H.D. Lee, 57 C.P.R. 60 (1981).

B. Vertical Externalities and the Importance of Performance Bonds

Klein and Murphy (1988), extending the model of Klein and Leffler (1981), present a vertical efficiency rationale for the use of RPM. In the Klein-Leffler model, firms use implicit and explicit contracts to create "performance bonds" for good behavior. For instance, a firm with a good whose quality is difficult to evaluate may invest in advertising to create a branded reputation for itself. This reputation creates for the firm a stream of quasi-rents that it receives as long as it continues to produce high-quality product. If it offers a lower quality product, it will receive short-run profits from selling a low quality good at a high quality price. Such "cheating", however, would cause the firm to lose the profits from its future stream of quasi-rents and would therefore be unprofitable. Thus, the performance bond of advertising insures product quality.

Klein and Murphy apply the Klein-Leffler model to vertical restraints. Retailers invest in the sale of a product. In exchange, the manufacturer gives the retailer a stream of quasi-rents in the form of RPM-induced margins. These margins are only available to the retailer, however, should it offer the manufacturer's product in a manner that the manufacturer desires. If the retailer "misbehaves" the manufacturer cuts off its supply of goods, thus denying the retailer the stream of RPM-induced quasi-rents. Klein and Murphy posit that vertical restraints can have one or more of four goals. First, they allow the manufacturer to induce non-price competition among its retailers, such as the provision of pre-sale information about complex goods. Second, they allow the manufacturer to purchase retailer promotional services. Third, they prevent dealers from being overcompensated for promotional services by manufacturers. Finally, they allow the manufacturer to control the type or number of dealers that sell its product.[5] In all these circumstances, vertical restraints prevent retailers from taking advantage of manufacturers by benefitting from vertical externalities.

---

[5] Using this analysis, Klein and Murphy argue that by reducing vertical externalities RPM can promote various forms of sales efforts, which are generally thought of as horizontal externalities. Discerning whether the provision of sales efforts is deterred by horizontal or vertical externalities is a debate this author does not wish to enter. Arbitrarily, for the rest of this paper I define the inducement of sales effort to be caused by a reduction in horizontal externalities.

Consider, for example, a franchisee of a nationally recognized fast-food chain. If the franchisee reduces the quality of its product below that desired by the national chain, it, in effect, "vertically free rides" on the national chain's reputation. By using RPM, the chain can punish the retailer for such behavior by cancelling its franchise contract and thus denying it a stream of RPM-induced quasi-rents. More broadly, the Klein and Murphy theory implies that RPM can be used to prevent retailers from using a manufacturer's reputation against the manufacturer's best interests. One of the important differences between Klein and Murphy and Telser is that while Telser's theory implies that RPM will be most useful for new products, Klein-Murphy implies that RPM will be of greatest use in protecting the reputation of established goods.

In an article that precedes the Klein-Murphy article but uses a similar form of analysis, Springer and Frech (1986) present a variant of the Klein-Leffler theory to explain RPM. They discuss how retailers have incentives to free-ride on brand names and deceive consumers.[6] Brand names are used to draw customers into the store. Once in the store, retailers then direct the customers to lower-quality unbranded products that offer larger returns to the retailer. Consumers thus believe that they are receiving high-quality branded products, or close substitutes, when in fact they are receiving low-quality products. Again, the threat of eliminating the supply of the manufacturer's good, and thus losing RPM-induced margins, can deter such behavior. This is similar to Klein and Murphy's (1988 at 286-7) argument that without RPM, "dealers will have the incentive to use their [manufacturers'] promotional efforts to switch marginal customers to other relatively unknown (unadvertised) brands that sell for a lower retail price, but which possess higher retail margins."

C. The Critics

The recent economic theories of RPM efficiencies have not been met with large favor by the Supreme Court or other parts of the legal community. While the *per se* prohibition on non-price

---

[6] If RPM and other vertical restraints are indeed used to reduce deception, it creates conflicting bureaucratic incentives for the FTC, an agency with the dual mission of antitrust and consumer protection enforcement.

vertical restraints laid down in United States v. Arnold. Schwinn & Co., 388 U.S. 365 (1967) was overruled in Continental T.V. Inc. v. GTE Sylvania Inc., 433 U.S. 36 (1977), the Court, while narrowing the definition of RPM along the lines of U.S. v. Colgate, 250 U.S. 300 (1919), expressly refused a Department of Justice invitation to overrule the RPM *per se* illegal standard in Monsanto v. Spray-Rite Service Corp., 465 U.S. 752 (1984). In Business Electronics v. Sharp Electronics, 485 U.S. 717 (1988), the Court, while reinforcing the "Colgate rule", reiterated its argument in Sylvania that "there was support for the proposition that vertical price restraints reduce interbrand competition because they facilitate cartelization."[7] The Court implicitly rejected the efficiency arguments for RPM, stating, "[i]n order to meet that interbrand competition, a manufacturer's dominant strategy is to lower resale prices."

Since Sharp, several bills have been reported out of the Senate Judiciary Committee to strengthen the *per se* ban on RPM.[8] In support of one of these bills former FTC Commissioner Robert Pitofsky stated (U.S. Senate Hearings, 1989 at 228) that "the `free rider' explanation for vertical price-fixing is a totally theoretical matter. No study has ever demonstrated that manufacturers regularly or frequently engage in minimum resale price-fixing to ensure provision of services, and many products as to which minimum price-fixing has been tried ... involve few if any services." In his opening statement to the Senate subcommittee (at 220), Pitofsky referred to the free-rider theory as "nonsense." Similarly, in a House hearing five years earlier, then-FTC Commissioner Patricia Bailey (U.S. House, 1984 at 43) stated, "[a]s a practical matter, the `free-rider' might be characterized as the Loch Ness Monster of Antitrust - everyone's heard of it, but except for an occasional shadowy outline, nobody's ever seen it." (For a further discussion, see Kelly, 1988.) In effect, both Pitofsky and Bailey have expressed their opinion that "free-riding" is largely the creation of theoretical economists.

---

[7] To justify its position, the Court referenced Posner (1974 at 134), Hellman (1984 at 498, fn. 12), and Gelhorn (1976 at 252, 256). These articles appear to discuss the cartel-enhancing properties of RPM only in theoretical terms. The cartel-enhancing properties of RPM are further discussed below in this Section.

[8] The chairman of the American Bar Association Section of Antitrust Law (Rosch, 1991 at 5) has referred to the Congressional attempts to overturn the case law as "*the* antitrust battle of the decade." (emphasis original)

In the economics profession itself, there is also doubt as to the validity and robustness of the free-rider arguments. For instance, a leading industrial organization textbook (Scherer and Ross, 1989 at 554) states that, "the free-rider justification of resale price maintenance has severe limitations. Its plausibility is palpably low in many product areas where RPM is used." Similarly, Adams and Brock (1990 at 227) assert that, "the `free rider' menace on which resale price maintenance defenders rely to rationalize vertical price-fixing turns out, on sober examination, to be more a figment of imagination than an empirical reality."[9]

Critics of the free-rider rationale usually focus on the traditional explanation given by Telser - free riding on pre-sale information for complex goods. They note that many or most RPM court cases involve products that are relatively simple. Thus, the criticisms have yet to deal with the less direct informational services provided by "shelf-space", as well as the relatively new Klein-Murphy rationale of vertical free-riding.

RPM's critics generally appear to believe that its primary usage is to generate collusive outcomes. There are two scenarios where this is projected to take place. In the first, a group of manufacturers use RPM as a device to facilitate their collusive scheme. RPM aids in collusion because retail prices are more observable than wholesale prices. In the second scenario, retailers collude and force manufacturers to use RPM to give retailers RPM-protected margins. Both scenarios have a number of theoretical difficulties.[10] In particular, both scenarios require that the group of manufacturers and/or retailers who use RPM jointly possess market power. The empirical evidence from litigation, generated by Ornstein (1985) and Ippolito (1991 at 281-2), indicates that this condition is not usually met.[11]

---

[9] From a legal viewpoint Blecher (1991 at 22) makes a similar argument, " ... the Chicago School's overriding concern with `point of sale' service and its potential elimination in the presence of free-riding discounters is grossly overstated. The need for extensive point of sale assistance and specialty marketing is limited to a relatively small number of technologically sophisticated or dangerous products. The rationale does not and should not be allowed to justify the wholesale elimination of discounters regardless of the product at issue."

[10] Steiner (1985) and Lynch (1986) also posit that RPM can be used in monopolistically competitive industries in order to deter the adoption of more efficient methods of retailing.

[11] Comanor (1985) argues that RPM and other vertical restraints can reduce welfare when the gains to one group of consumers through the supplied services is less than the loses to the "inframarginal" consumers who do not desire the service. White (1985) notes a large number of problems with this argument. In addition, the argument

7

III. The Early Case Law

A. The Changing Rule of Law

The case law in the English-speaking world on restraint of trade is quite old. (Peppin, 1940 at 310, fn. 43, cites a case dating back to 1298.) In this context, RPM cases are relatively new. Seligman and Love (1932 at 22) report an undefined 1775 RPM "incident" involving an English bookseller. The 1917 FTC Hearings (at 511) discuss an 1852 English Commission, with Charles Dickens as a member, that reviewed RPM in the bookselling industry. Bowman (1955 at 826) states that the first use of RPM in the U.S., by drug wholesalers, occurred in 1875. The first reported American RPM litigation is Clark v. Frank, 17 Mo. Appeal 602 (1885), a Missouri case involving a thread company's imposition of RPM. Given the long history of antitrust jurisprudence, it seems odd that RPM arose as a legal matter in the English-speaking world only in the late 19th century.[12]

Table 1 lists the pre-1918 federal case law.[13] Prior to 1907 "vertical" RPM (defined here as RPM imposed without an agreement between competing manufacturers) appears to have been virtually *per se* legal, at least at the Federal level. For instance, Judge Acheson wrote in Edison v. Kaufman (105 F. at 960), "I cannot doubt that the complainants have the right to sell their patented phonograph with ... [price] restrictions." While striking down a RPM plan involving an agreement by horizontal rivals in Jayne v. Loder (149 F. at 27), Judge Archibald stated, "Undoubtedly the originator and compounder of a proprietary medicine may shape his own policy, and sell or withhold from selling, as he pleases, according to supposed self-interest or whim;

---

requires that the manufacturer imposing the vertical restraint possess unilateral market power. Again, empirically this is not usually the case.

[12] See Bittlingmayer (1988) for a discussion of the 18th century experience with RPM in the German bookselling market.

[13] A list of 42 cases is contained in Seligman and Love (1932 at 476-7). Forty of these cases clearly involved RPM. One of the cases, N.J. Patents v. Weinberg (1910, C.C.PA.) appears to be unpublished. The text of N.J. Patents v. Martin 166 F. 1010 (1909) is too terse from which to support any conclusions. (The discussion in N.J. Patents v. Schaeffer 178 F. 276 indicates that the New Jersey Patent Company produced gramophones.) I found 3 additional cases mentioned in Bowman (1955). I searched other cases referred to in the Congressional hearings and found 6 additional RPM cases.

Table One

Federal RPM Cases Prior To 1918

Parties	Final Case Citation	Year	Plaintiff	Product	Product Type	District Court	Outcome For RPM	Appeals Circuit	Appeals Outcome	Supreme Court	S.C. Vote
Fowle v. Park	131 U.S. 88	1889	Manufacturer	Medicine	Simple	S.D. Ohio	Lost			Won	9 to 0
Bowling v. Taylor	40 F. 404	1889	Patent Owner	Dress Stays	Simple	Conn.	Won				
U.S. v. Greenhut	51 F. 205	1892	U.S.	Liquor	Simple	N.D. Ohio	Won				
In re Greene	52 F. 104	1892	Wholesaler	Liquor	Simple	S.D. Ohio	Won				
Edison v. Kaufman	105 F. 960	1901	Manufacturer	Gramophone	Complex	W.D. Pa	Won				
Bement v. Harrow	186 U.S. 70	1902	Manufacturer	Agric. Implement	Complex?	N.Y. State	Lost		Won	Won	6 to 0
Edison v. Pike	116 F. 863	1902	Manufacturer	Gramophone	Complex	Mass.	Won				
Victor v. The Fair	123 F. 424	1903	Manufacturer	Gramophone	Complex	N.D. Ill.	Lost	7	Won		
Natl. Phonograph v. Schlegel	128 F. 732	1904	Manufacturer	Gramophone	Complex	S.D. Iowa	Lost	8	Won		
Bobbs-Merrill v. Snellenburg	131 F. 530	1904	Manufacturer	Books	Simple?	E.D. PA	Lost				
Dr. Miles v. Goldthwaite	133 F. 794	1904	Manufacturer	Medicine	Simple	Mass.	Won				
In re Park	138 F. 422	1905	Manufacturer	Medicine	Simple	S.D. Ohio	Won				
Dr. Miles v. Platt	142 F. 606	1906	Manufacturer	Medicine	Simple	N.D. Ill.	Won				
Dispensary Med. Assn. v. Platt	142 F. 606	1906	Manufacturer	Medicine	Simple	N.D. Ill.	Won				
Hartman's v. Platt	142 F. 606	1906	Manufacturer	Medicine	Simple	N.D. Ill.	Won				
Author's Assn. v. O'Gorman	147 F. 616	1906	Manufacturer	Books	Simple?	R.I.	Won				
Wells & Richardson v. Abraham	146 F. 190	1906	Manufacturer	Medicine	Simple	E.D. N.Y.	Won				
Ingersoll v. Snellenberg	147 F. 522	1906	Wholesaler	Watches	Simple	E.D. PA	Split				

Table One (Continued)

Federal RPM Cases Prior To 1918

Parties	Final Case Citation	Year	Plaintiff	Product	Product Type	District Court	Outcome For RPM	Appeals Circuit	Outcome	Supreme Court	S.C. Vote
Jayne v. Loder	149 F. 21	1906	Retailer	Medicine	Simple	E.D. PA.	Lost	3	Lost		
Dr. Miles v. Jaynes Drug	149 F. 838	1906	Manufacturer	Medicine	Simple	Mass.	Won				
Park v. Hartman	153 F. 24	1907	Manufacturer	Medicine	Simple	E.D. KY	Won	6	Lost		
Rubber Tire v. Milw. Rubber	154 F. 358	1907	Patent Owner	Auto. Tires	Simple?	E.D. Wisc.	Lost	7	Won		
Ind. Mfg. v. Case Threshing	154 F. 365	1907	Patent Owner	Threshing Mach.	Complex	E.D. Wisc.	Lost	7	Won		
Bobbs-Merrill v. Straus	210 U.S. 339	1908	Manufacturer	Books	Simple?	S.D. N.Y.	Lost	2	Lost	Lost	9 to 0
Scribner v. Straus	210 U.S. 352	1908	Manufacturer	Books	Simple?	S.D. N.Y.	Lost	2	Lost	Lost	9 to 0
The Fair v. Dover	166 F. 117	1908	Manufacturer	Irons	Complex?	E.D. Ill.	Won	7	Won		
N.J. Patent v. Schaefer	178 F. 276	1909	Manufacturer	Gramophone	Complex	E.D. PA	Won	3	Won		
Dr. Miles v. Park	220 U.S. 373	1911	Manufacturer	Medicine	Simple	E.D. KY	Lost	6	Lost	Lost	7 to 1
Pencil Sharpening v. Goldsmith	190 F. 205	1911	Manufacturer	Pencil Sharpeners	Simple?	N.D. N.Y.	Won				
Edison v. Smith	188 F. 925	1911	Manufacturer	Gramophone	Complex	W.D. MI	Won				
Winchester v. Buengar	199 F. 786	1912	Manufacturer	Armaments	Complex	E.D. Wisc.	Won				
Henry v. A.B. Dick	224 U.S. 1	1912	Manufacturer	Mimeograph	Complex	S.D. N.Y.	Won	2	Passed	Won	4 to 3
Standard Sanitary v. U.S.	226 U.S. 20	1912	U.S.	Iron Ware	Simple	Maryland	Lost			Lost	9 to 0
Lovell-McCon. v. Intl. Auto.	202 F. 219	1913	Manufacturer	Auto. Horns	Simple	W.D. N.Y.	Won	2	Won		
Winchester v. Olmstead	203 F. 493	1913	Manufacturer	Armaments	Complex?	N.D. Ill.	Lost	7	Won		

Table One (Continued)

Federal RPM Cases Prior To 1918

Parties	Final Case Citation	Year	Plaintiff	Product	Product Type	District Court	Outcome For RPM	Appeals Circuit	Outcome	Supreme Court	S.C. Vote
Ingersoll v. McColl	204 F. 147	1913	Manufactuer	Watches	Simple	Minn.	Lost				
Waltham Watch v. Keene	202 F. 225	1913	Manufacturer	Watches	Simple	S.D. N.Y.	Lost				
Free Sewing v. Bry-Block	204 F. 632	1913	Manufacturer	Sewing Mach.	Complex	W.D. TN	Lost				
Bauer v. O'Donnell	229 U.S. 1	1913	Manufacturer	Medicine	Simple	D.C.	Lost	D.C.	Passed	Lost	5 to 4
U.S. v. Keystone Watch	218 F. 502	1915	U.S.	Watches	Simple	E.D. PA	Split				
U.S. v. Kellogg Corn Flakes	222 F. 725	1915	U.S.	Cereal	Simple	E.D. MI	Lost				
A & P v. Cream of Wheat	224 F. 566	1915	Retailer	Cereal	Simple	S.D. N.Y.	Won				
U.S. v. Eastman Kodak	226 F. 62	1915	U.S.	Cameras	Complex	W.D. N.Y.	Lost				
Waterman v. Kline	234 F. 891	1916	Manufacturer	Pens	Simple	N.D. WV	Won	4	Won		
Victor v. Strauss	243 U.S. 490	1917	Manufacturer	Gramophone	Complex	S.D. N.Y.	Lost	2	Won	Lost	6 to 3
Ford v. Union Motor Sales	225 F. 373	1917	Manufacturer	Automobiles	Complex	S.D. Ohio	Lost				
Ford v. Boone	244 F. 22	1917	Manufacturer	Automobiles	Complex	Oregon	Lost	9	Won		
Boston Store v. Amer. Gram.	225 F. 785 (246 U.S. 6 1918)	1917	Manufacturer	Gramophone	Complex	N.D. Ill	Won	7	Passed	Lost	7 to 2
Frey v. Welch Grape Juice	240 F. 114 (261 F. 68 1919)	1917	Wholesaler	Grape Juice	Simple	Maryland	Lost	4	Lost		

Cases notes: Fowle v. Park was decided before Appeals Courts were established in 1891. Bement v. Harrow reached the Supreme Court on appeal from the New York State court sytem. The three appeals court decisions marked "passed" denote when the Appeals Court submitted questions to the Supreme Court on the relevant case without making its own decision. The "Split" referred to in Bobbs-Merrill v. Snellenburg and U.S. v. Keystone Watch are District Court decisions which state it was legal for the firms to impose RPM on their wholesalers, but not to impose it on retailers who received those goods from the wholesalers. Thirty-six of the plaintiffs were manufacturers seeking to enforce their RPM contracts, 3 were patent owners seeking to enforce contracts, three were wholesalers attempted to escape contracts, as were two cases brought by retailers. Five cases were brought by the U.S. Department of Justice. Twenty-four of the District Court decisions found for RPM, 23 found against, and two were split. Twelve of the Appeals Court decisions supported RPM, six opposed, and three courts passed the decision to the Supreme Court. Three of the Supreme Court decision supported RPM and 7 opposed.

fixing the prices and naming the terms at and upon which alone he will do so, refusing to those who will not comply. And so far as this is confined to his own goods, and pursued by independent and individual action, it cannot be challenged."

RPM was struck down in only three of the 19 pre-1907 cases. In <u>Bobbs-Merrill v. Snellenberg</u> (1904) the District Court ruled that RPM notices in the copyrights of books did not create binding contracts with retailers. In <u>Jayne v. Loder</u> (1906) the District and Appellate Courts ruled against a horizontal conspiracy among home remedy companies in the Philadelphia region that imposed RPM on all retailers and wholesalers in the area. <u>Jayne v. Loder</u> would appear to be the classic RPM rule-of-reason case, as it appears that the relevant manufacturers together may have had market power and could have been using RPM to facilitate collusion.[14] In <u>Ingersoll v. Snellenberg</u> (1906) the District Court ruled that, while a contract could impose RPM on the immediate recipient of a good, it could not force that recipient to impose RPM on subsequent buyers.[15]

The legal turning point for RPM was <u>Park v. Hartman</u> (1907). In this decision then-Appellate Court Judge Lurton wrote that RPM was an illegal restraint-of-trade because it eliminated what is now referred to as "intra-brand competition." Lurton stated in his ruling that while the owner of a copyright could not engage in RPM, an owner of a patent could due to the monopoly rights that the patent granted.

Between 1908 and 1917 RPM law was in a state of flux.[16] In 1908 the Supreme Court in <u>Bobbs-Merrill v. Straus</u> and its companion case <u>Scribner v. Straus</u> ruled that copyrights notices did not constitute valid RPM contracts in fact situations similar to that in <u>Bobbs-Merrill v. Snellenberg</u>. In 1910 Lurton joined the Supreme Court. While Lurton did not participate in the famous 1911 <u>Dr. Miles</u> decision, Justice Hughes' decision largely echoes Lurton's previous Appellate Court

---

[14] It is conceptually possible that multilateral RPM may be necessary to deter free-riding on special services for complex goods. For instance, assume that there are several producers of VCR's, each producing very similar products. If only one firm imposes RPM, the other firms can free ride on the services that firm's retailers provide.

[15] Thus, under this decision the Ingersoll Watch Company could impose RPM directly on its wholesalers but could not enter into contracts with its wholesalers that would force them to impose RPM on their retailers.

[16] Seligman and Love (1932 at 23) refer to this era in RPM law as "The Period of Uncertainty."

rulings. (Dr. Miles was decided on a 7-1 vote, with Holmes dissenting.) Yet the next year in A.B. Dick, consistent with his Park v. Hartman decision, Lurton switched sides, writing for the plurality in a 4-3 decision upholding RPM on patented goods.[17] In the 1913 case Bauer v. O'Donnell, Justice Day wrote the 5-4 majority opinion striking down vertical RPM on patented goods. (The majority included newly seated Justice Pitney). The four justices who made up the plurality in A.B. Dick voted against the Bauer decision without writing a dissent.

In 1914 Lurton died and was replaced by Attorney General McReynolds. In 1916 Justice Lamar, part of the Bauer majority, died and Justice Hughes resigned from the court to accept the Republican nomination for President. Lamar and Hughes were replaced by Brandeis, an RPM supporter,[18] and Clarke, who appears not to have had any previous position on the issue. Thus, by 1917 the court apparently consisted of three strong opponents of RPM (Day, White, and Pitney), two justices who had taken contrary positions (McKenna and Van Devanter, who were in the anti-RPM majority in Dr. Miles, the pro-RPM plurality in A.B. Dick, and the pro-RPM minority in Bauer), two strong RPM supporters (Brandeis and Holmes), and two justices who had not yet taken a position on the issue (McReynolds[19] and Clarke). In April 1917 the court decided against vertical RPM on patented goods 6-3 in Straus v. Victor, with Day writing the opinion, Brandeis, Clarke and McReynolds joining the majority, and McKenna, Holmes, and Van Devanter dissenting once more. During the period between 1911 and 1918 five appellate court decisions ruled in favor of vertical RPM, three passed the decision on to the Supreme Court,[20] while only one appellate court decision found against vertical RPM.

---

[17] One seat was open, and Day did not participate. The discussion of the case implies that the matter at hand dealt with tying. Lurton and Hughes (dissenting), however, took the opportunity to discuss the legality of RPM on trademark goods (Dr. Miles) compared to RPM on patent goods (A.B. Dick).

[18] Brandeis' support for the RPM legalization campaign is discussed in McCraw (1984 at 101-106).

[19] McReynolds may have played a role in the initial part of the Justice Department's prosecution of the 1915 Kellogg, Keystone, and Kodak cases (see Table 1).

[20] During this time, under the Court of Appeals Act of 1891, Appeals Courts could request instruction on cases from the Supreme Court.

Judicial hopes for RPM were finally dashed in 1918, when, responding to questions from a 7th Circuit Court that passed on a District court decision upholding an RPM contract, the Supreme Court struck down a vertical RPM plan by a 7-2 vote in Boston Store v. American Gramophone. In Boston Store McKenna switched sides and Brandeis issued a concurring opinion stating that while he believed RPM should be legal, its illegality was now a matter of settled law. Given this judicial turmoil, it seems that during the years 1915 to 1917 it was unclear exactly what the next Supreme Court decision on RPM would generate.

The period 1908 to 1917 was therefore a crucial period for RPM. Before 1908 RPM was not an issue, as it appears to have been legal. Thus, there was no reason for RPM advocates to make the case for the efficiency of the practice. After 1917 RPM was clearly *per se* illegal. As Easterbrook (1984 at 6-7) points out, "[o]nce a practice has been declared unlawful, a business is likely to defend a lawsuit by denying that it engaged in that practice. Rarely will it say `Yes, we did that, and here is why it is economically beneficial that we did.'" Thus, at least in a legal context, firms would find it difficult to argue the efficiency aspects of RPM. Indeed, in her study of 203 RPM cases brought between 1976 and 1982, Ippolito (1991 at 68-9) found no evidence of any attempts by defendants to mount an efficiency defense. Further, once the practice was declared illegal, firms would be unlikely to go into public forums and argue the efficiencies of existing RPM arrangements, because to do so would be to invite government and private lawsuits. Thus, these ten years represent a period where private parties who actually engaged in RPM would have the incentives to articulate RPM's efficiency properties.

B. The Goods and the Issues in the Early Litigation

The cases themselves involved a variety of products. As discussed above, the Telser special services argument applies best to new and complicated products, like VCRs in the 1980s. Of course, VCRs did not exist prior to 1918. But what may be considered the VCR's linear antecedent, the gramophone, did. Gramophones were involved in eight of the 49 pre-1918 cases. Two of the cases involved Ford automobiles, also a new and complicated good in the pre-1918 era. Other complicated goods in Table 1 are cameras, mimeographs, sewing machines, and threshing machines. Armaments (two cases), irons, and agricultural implements[21] may have been complicated goods during this time period. Over-the-counter medicines were represented in 12 cases. The Marvel and McCafferty (1984) story seems most appropriate for medicines, with consumers looking to retailers for certification of quality for very uncertain home remedies. Book-sellers, whose efficiency motivations for RPM are discussed in Bittlingmayer (1988), represent four cases. Three cases dealt with apparently highly branded goods (Kellogg's Corn Flakes, Cream of Wheat cereal and Welch's grape juice). Four cases involved watches. Other cases involving apparently simple goods dealt with automobile horns, automobile tires, dress stays, iron ware, liquor, pencil sharpeners, and pens.

In general, RPM opponents in the judiciary presented two arguments. The first, made originally by Lurton in 1907 and echoed by Hughes in Dr. Miles, was that RPM reduced intra-brand competition. The second, presented by Hughes in Dr. Miles, asserted that once a firm sold a particular good, it had no further legitimate interest in that good. Only two of these cases, Jayne v. Loder and Standard Sanitary v. U.S. (1912), discuss any type of interbrand collusive arrangement that appears to be the current rationale for the legal opposition to RPM.[22]

Most of the plaintiffs in these cases were manufacturers or patent holders attempting to enforce RPM contracts with their distributors, retailers, or licensees. Of the 28 cases up to and including Dr. Miles, 26 were brought by parties desiring to enforce RPM restrictions. Even after Dr. Miles, from 1911 to 1917, 16 of the 21 cases were brought by manufacturers seeking to uphold RPM contracts. Unlike Ippolito (1991 at 269, examining cases from a later period), I did

---

[21] The good involved in Benment v. National Harrow was a harrow, which my dictionary defines as "a wheelless agricultural implement set with teeth, upright disks, etc., usually of iron, drawn over plowed land to level it, break clods, etc."

[22] While there was little discussion of the anti-competitive effects of RPM in the case law, there was almost no discussion of RPM's potential efficiency aspects. The only real attempt to discuss such efficiencies was part of one paragraph in Holmes' dissent in Dr. Miles. Holmes expressed part of his disagreement with the majority by stating (at 412), "I cannot believe that in the long run the public will profit by this court permitting knaves to cut reasonable prices for some ulterior purpose of their own and thus to impair, if not destroy, the production and sale of articles which it is assumed to be desirable that the public get." This argument, while consistent with modern efficiency stories, does not clearly articulate any particular theory.

not find any cases that dealt with maximum RPM, though courts during this period may not have noted the differences in types of RPM.

IV. Efficiencies Articulated

Early supporters of RPM had two different national forums to present reasons why the Supreme Court decisions in Dr. Miles and Bauer should have been overturned, either by the courts or by Congress. The first occurred in hearings held by the Committee on Interstate and Foreign Commerce of the House of Representatives in 1915, 1916, and 1917 ("Hearings I", "Hearings II", and "Hearings III") on Representative Dan V. Stephens' (Nebraska) bill to permit RPM on trademarked goods. These hearings produced a mixed selection of pro- and anti-RPM statements. While Stephens and other representatives clearly supported RPM, the committee chairman, William C. Adamson (Georgia) was opposed. Adamson's position was supported in the committee by two then-rising stars of the Democratic party, future Speaker of the House Sam Rayburn (Texas) and future Senator and Vice-President Alben Barkley (Kentucky).

The second forum was seven days of hearings the FTC held in October and November of 1917 ("FTC"). The commission had brought its first series of RPM complaints in 1917. It then invited its respondents to a conference to explain their efficiency rationales for RPM. The FTC hearings largely, though not entirely, involved RPM proponents.[23] The purpose of the hearing, according to Commissioner Fort (FTC at 1009) was "simply to allow the respondents in these twenty-eight cases to appear and to talk generally on the general subject."[24]

---

[23] These hearings were apparently never published by the FTC. I found the approximately 1300 pages of hearing transcript in the FTC library. About 20 percent of the transcript is unreadable due to faded carbons. Tosdale (1918 at 28) reports that much of the transcript was published in *Women's Wear Daily*. The hearings did not cause the Commission to discontinue its opposition to RPM.

[24] Economists do not seem to have had a large impact on framing the efficiency arguments for RPM. As Breit (1991) points out, most economists during this period were opposed to RPM. Professor Lee Galloway of New York University and Professor Paul H. Nystrom, formerly of University of Wisconsin and the University of Minnesota, spoke in favor of RPM during the hearings, but neither's analysis was particularly sophisticated. RPM opponents often cited Taussig (1916) and the text of that article was inserted into the record of the 1916 House Hearings (at 266-277). Stephens, the sponsor of the RPM bills, indicated (Hearings III at 412) that most economists opposed his proposal.

A. National Advertising

As noted above, with the exception of the book trade, RPM does not appear to have been used prior to 1875. The hearings offered an answer to that puzzle. It appears that the factor that instigated the use of RPM was the rise of national advertising.[25] For instance, Edmund E. Wise, Counsel for Straus[26] stated (Hearings III at 5):

> Now, price maintenance, so called, is a matter of comparatively recent origin. It is the offspring of national advertising, as distinguished from local advertising. The parties who developed national advertising were the druggists, to a large extent the proprietors of pharmaceutical preparations.

Wise had a chance to press his point, when, sitting in the audience at the FTC hearing, he asked William H. Ingersoll of Ingersoll Watch Company (an RPM proponent and the plaintiff in two of the RPM cases in Table 1) why this system had arisen only in the previous 40 years (FTC at 70). According to Ingersoll

> [Prior to that time] the old craftsman ... had a very local and small trade ... We are talking of conditions today.
>
> Wise: By which you mean national advertising being the basis of the new system.
>
> Ingersoll: I would not say it is the basis. It is an element of it.

A similar opinion was voiced by Colonel Ned A. Flood of Cluett, Peabody & Co., manufacturers of Arrow Collars (FTC at 186):

> Twenty-five or thirty years ago there was not in the collar industry in the United States anything resembling in the remotest degree the branded or trade-marked collar which we recognize today as one of the potential factors in the industry. The branded article, the trade-marked article came into being precisely, almost concurrently, with the art of advertising. There is no question about that. The trade-marked, the branded article is the article that today has a nation-wide, if you

---

[25] Following sections will discuss how the firms that created these brand names argued that they needed RPM to protect their investments against both horizontal and vertical forms of free-riding.

[26] Strauss was the parent company of Macy's department store. Tosdale (1918 at 32, fn. 13) notes that Straus was "one of the most prominent opponents of legalized price maintenance." Wise was the victorious counsel in the three RPM Supreme Court decisions where Straus was the defendant.

please, in some instances a world-wide reputation known generally everywhere. How is it made known? Through the agency of publicity.

Perhaps the best evidence that RPM was largely a function of national advertising comes from parties who suffered at the hands of national advertising, local newspapers dependant on local advertising. According to Harry B. Haines, the publisher of the Paterson (N.J.) *Evening News* (Hearings III at 90-91):[27]

> ... in my opinion, this bill [the Stephens bill], as it now stands, if passed, would result within a very few months after its passage in a more serious loss to the newspaper publishers of the smaller cities of the United States than any measure of its kind that could possibly be conceived. It is a matter of record in our newspaper, and the newspapers of other cities of like size,... that about 80 per cent of our advertising is local advertising. ... I am of the firm conviction that this bill, had it been entitled instead ... a bill to discourage and eliminate local advertising in newspapers, it might have perhaps been better named.

The participants appeared united in their belief that such publications as the *Saturday Evening Post* and *Ladies' Home Journal*, which had attained large national distributions in the 1880s, had opened up new opportunities for the creation of nationally recognized brand names.

Advertising generated brand names, which were a new phenomenon in the economy. Both Congressmen and FTC Commissioners asked questions about the economic value of brand names. These questions led to several fairly sophisticated discussions of the economic effects of these marketing tools. Consider, for example, the following exchange between Sol Westerfeld (unidentified, but apparently a businessman) and Congressman Samuel Winslow (Massachusetts) (Hearings II at 129):

> Winslow: What value do you put on the reputation [of a trade-mark]-its value in connection with the article?
>
> Westerfeld: All that the article merits-no more nor less.
>
> Winslow: Then you think it is valuable to some one?

---

[27] The publisher of the *New York Globe*, Jason Rogers, made a similar statement in the FTC hearings (at 437).

Westerfeld: Yes, sir.

Winslow: But not to the consumer?

Westerfeld: It is, because it helps the consumer to select certain merchandise which otherwise would cause him to grope in the dark, but he does not pay any special price for it.

Winslow: Does it not mean that it is an insurance of quality

Westerfeld: Yes, sir.

Mrs. Julian Heath, National President of the National Housewives League (Hearings II at 187), stated it more concisely: "[t]he label is the housewife's only identification of quality, purity, sanitation, quantity, [and] standardization." Future Supreme Court Justice Louis Brandeis, in a piece entitled, "Cutthroat Prices - The Competition That Kills" in *Harper's Weekly* for Nov. 15, 1913 (cited in Hearings II at 244), discussing the establishment of stores that sold goods at market prices, articulated the bonding characteristics of reputation:

> Under such conditions the purchaser had still to rely for protection on his own acumen, or on the character and judgement of the retailer, and the individual. The unscrupulous or unskilful dealer might be led to abandon his goods for cheaper and inferior substitutes. This ever-present danger led to an ever-widening use of trade-marks. Thereby the producer secured the reward for well doing and the consumer the desired guarantee of quality.

Using this type of analysis, proponents of RPM refuted Justice Hughes' assertion in Dr. Miles that a manufacturer has no interest in a good once it has been sold. For instance William Ingersoll argued (FTC at 47)

> When a grocer buys his Ivory soap he buys the physical commodity and that he owns and it belongs to him and he can do whatever he pleases with that, just as the Supreme Court said he could. But who would contend that the Ivory brand, worth millions of dollars, belongs to him when he buys a dozen bars of soap. It does not, of course. That good-will belongs to the Ivory people. They create it, they own it; it is theirs and on the same doctrine that the man can do what he pleases with what he owns why cannot the Ivory soap people do what they please with what they own?

J. George Frederick, Editor, *Advertising/Selling Magazine* (FTC at 549) expressed a similar opinion.

> It appears to me, as a matter of fact, that advertising has a very remarkable relation to this entire subject of price maintenance, in the first place, by reason of the fact that the part of the commodity which is not merely material, but which is intangible, the good will, in other words, which is developed wholly and only by advertising and reputation making devices and experiences which are really advertising constitute the central point and pivot of the entire subject.

These arguments are all components of the Klein-Leffler story of advertising acting as a bonding mechanism for product quality, which was written more than 60 years later.

The origins of RPM may also describe something about its purpose. The roots of horizontal restraints would appear to be the desire for collusive outcomes. Since the root of RPM in the United States was national advertising, it may imply that something to do with national advertising, not collusion, was the source of the desire to implement RPM.

B. Inducing Sales Efforts

One of the horizontal externality explanations for vertical restraints was to increase cooperation and "sales effort" from retailers. In effect, RPM encourages retailers to devote more of their resources (both salesmen's time and shelf space) to selling a particular good. This story was articulated quite well by RPM supporters. For instance, according to a letter from A.L. Fry of St. Louis, Missouri (Hearings I at 115):

> The price cutting which is practiced on our goods throughout the country is causing us endless inconveniences and trouble and, most important of all, losses of sales, as the prices are cut to such an extent by the department stores and some of the large drug stores that the small dealer is very reluctant to handle our product, and he is only too glad, when a customer asks for Kolynos Dental Cream, to substitute something else if he can possibly do it.
>   During the month of August we sent to the retail drug trade a card offering a counter display stand and samples of Kolynos Dental Cream. Quite a large number of these cards were returned to us with the following remarks: "We don't display 25 cent preparations that are cut to 16 cents."

Congressman Perl Decker (Missouri) gave an account of his personal experience along these lines (Hearings II at 38):

> As a retail salesman I was trained by my employer on how to substitute goods we preferred to sell when customers asked for something we did not want to carry. We kept the disliked articles under the counter, out of sight, and kept the other things in sight, well displayed. When a customer came in and asked for, we will say, corn flakes, if we did not care to sell him Blank's corn flakes, we would immediately get out a package of some other corn flakes. If the customers asked for Blank's Corn Flakes, we would go and get him the package, place it on the counter and begin to wrap it up and then say to the customer, "Madam, have you ever tried So-and-So's Corn Flakes!" And the customer might say, "No." Our reply would be, "Well, we find them very satisfactory and shall be very glad if you will try them at some time." In most cases the customer says, "Well if you say they are good, I'll try them now." In this way we succeeded in shifting the customer from the disliked article to the article we desired to sell, and all the advertising done by Blank's Corn Flakes wouldn't help him unless we let it help him. Without the dealer's good will, the manufacturer's advertising is wasted.

Note that the last sentence of Decker's statement implies that advertising and "shelf space" are complements. This may help explain why RPM arose after the advent of national advertising.

A letter to the FTC from the President and Chairman of the Legislative Committee of the Wholesale Grocers of Ohio (FTC at 84-85) supported RPM for a combination of reasons concerning horizontal free-riding on shelf space and vertical free-riding on brands:

> Under any other condition the consumer is liable to be deprived of the opportunity to obtain many desired commodities which are used by certain unscrupulous dealers only for the purpose of drawing trade at the expense of the advertising of the manufacturer. When this takes place legitimate dealers are compelled to push the sales of competing goods, sometimes refusing to handle the advertised goods which may be of better value to the consumer. Also, the manufacturer of the specialty advertised article has invested capital in the goods and the advertising which he cannot protect unless he is permitted to dictate the minimum price to consumer.

At least one participant felt that buying marketing effort was the impetus behind RPM in the home remedy industry. Discussing such products, Dr. William C. Anderson, representing the Conference of Independent Retail Druggists of New York (Hearings III at 506) stated:

> Prior to the introduction of cut prices on these articles they were subject to general distribution in the drug stores. The druggist received a legitimate profit on the sale

of these things. They were put on his counters and his shelves, window displays were made of them, and they were placed before the public in such a way as to benefit the manufacturer in the sale of those things. The druggist was interested in their sale. But when those things were cut to such an extent that it was a matter of handing the article over the counter and losing money on every package sold, those packages were placed in a cupboard or in a back shelf, and where formerly dozens were kept on hand there were one or two bottles kept, and they were sold only on demand and pressure.

Thus, consistent with Goldberg (1984) and Bittlingmayer (1988), these actors saw RPM as a method of manufacturers buying "shelf space" and promotional activity for their products, increasing the marketing activities that retailers engaged in. Further, if national advertising and shelf space were complements (which appears to be the case today), it would help explain why the desire for RPM was generated by national advertising.[28]

C. Free-Riding on Direct Information

RPM is also postulated to be used to prevent free-riding on direct information provided by retailers. This theory was also well articulated in the hearings. According to RPM supporter Christine Frederick, Consulting Home Editor of *Ladies' Home Journal* (Hearings II at 160),

> the retailer stands in relation to the consumer as an information bureau as to what she is going to buy.... I go to my retailer who is specializing in one line and consider him an information bureau who is going to, with his fuller knowledge and length of practice in the industry, give me the benefit of his experience.

Two very similar exchanges took place on this point, the first in the 1916 Hearings (at 91) between Congressman Barkley and Charles Dushkind of the Tobacco Merchant's Association:

> Congressman Barkley: How is there to be competition between the retailers if they do not compete as to prices? What other elements will enter?

---

[28] In a leading advertising text of the early part of this century, Cherington (1976, first published in 1913) devotes a good deal of effort to arguing that advertising and shelf space are complements. For example, in a chapter on RPM, Cherington (at 384) quotes one source as stating, "The advertising man ought to know what profit the dealer makes, and what profit he ought to make, for this reason if no other. He doesn't want to be placed in a position where he is going ahead creating demand for goods which is being filled with somebody's private brand."

Dushkind: Simply the personal element-the personal treatment you receive. You go to the nearest cigar store, to the man who is your friend or neighbour.

The next year in the FTC hearings (at 263-4) Commissioner Murdock had the following dialogue

with Keen H. Addington of the Benjamin Electric Manufacturing Company

Murdock: There had been a great deal of eloquence expended here as to the selling facilities of national advertising. No one had spoken a single word with reference to the facility with which the retail clerk enjoys as a good salesman. Suppose your proposition is carried out in its entirety and price maintenance is permitted, and everything that a retailer has in his store -- and this is a retailer who carries a variety of articles -- the price of everything in his store is fixed for him: precisely what is his function in the community?

Addington: He is an agent or distributor of what he has on his shelves.

Murdock: His quality of salesmanship is completely eliminated?

Addington: No, because he will have many competing articles on his shelves. He is a man who has dealt in all of them; he is well versed on the merits of each of them; he is a local man who deals with his friends; he will be very frank and honest in explaining the good points of one and the bad points of another.

Finally, there were book-sellers, from apparently the first industry to use RPM, speaking at the

hearings. Charles E. Butler of Brentano's (a book publisher) (FTC at 1030-1) argued that RPM

was needed so that booksellers could give advice to their customers on which books to buy:

Now gentlemen, here is where a great injury comes, caused by the predatory price cutters; of books so cut, the dealer tries to avoid keeping. If he does so he keeps a copy or so under his counter to supply some particular customer. To others he has not got it. Carefully note the following fact. It is proved that fully 75 per cent of a bookseller[']s sales of new books are sold on his recommendation and suggestion to the public, not more than 25 per cent being asked for by the public. Thus, the public entering the store to buy would not be shown or solicited to buy the cut book, but some other would be substituted if possible that would yield profit. And so it was, throughout the entire stock.

The public suffered greatly from the poor service given, the small and dwindling stock, sold stock was replaced as little as possible. Proprietors, clerks, and all classes of employees suffered. Efficient and expensive help were dispensed with, their places being filled by the most inefficient and cheapest. The utmost economy was practised, in fact, the entire booktrade was virtually dead.

Thus, these participants saw RPM as generating rewards for retailers acting as "information bureaus," advising customers on which products to purchase.

D. Free-Riding on Special Services For Complex Goods

Section III discusses how much of the early RPM litigation dealt with the new products of gramophones and automobiles. The inventor Thomas Edison, who also operated a gramophone company that was the plaintiff in three of the cases in Table 1, sent representatives to the House and FTC hearings. An article by Edison, which appeared in *Leslie's Weekly*, was inserted into the Hearings I record (at 196)

> When the inventor [of a product] approaches these jobbers and dealers he is told that if he wants them to sell his goods he must not only protect the price; he must set a price which will afford a profit consistent with the labor required to introduce and sell new things since they (the jobbers and the dealers) must invest in something the demand for which is unknown, and which, in any event, it will take a long time to create a large demand for, because the public must be educated to its advantages; If the inventor is not allowed to maintain the price at which the public is to obtain the invention, the jobbers and dealers will not handle his goods.

Thus, Edison argued that innovators needed their products to have the retail margins RPM provided in order for retailers to bear the cost of educating consumers on how to use its products. This is no different than the desire of a modern manufacturer to use RPM to teach consumers how to use its VCRs. One of Edison's competitors, Henry C. Brown of the Victor Talking Machine Company (plaintiff in two of the Table 1 cases and the loser earlier in the year in the Supreme Court decision Victor v. Straus), explained to the FTC (at 805-6) the in-store amenities that RPM (together with the use of exclusive dealing) allowed:

> But today you can go into probably 75 to 125 different stores scattered throughout the City of Chicago and its environs and make your choice of Victor records in the most beautiful environments. There are a number of the most beautiful and exclusive stores who are specializing in presenting them, and which offer an opportunity for the various customers to hear them under the most advantageous conditions, etc. If, as has been contended here, the prices of our goods cannot be maintained, I say to you frankly, gentlemen, that every one of the individual stores that make a living out of Victor Talking Machines exclusively would have to close.

A wholesaler and retailer of Victor gramophones, J. Newcomb Blackman, President of Blackman

Talking Machine Company, supported RPM in his market by arguing

> The talking machine business should be referred to as a specialty line, and, particularly in the case of the Victor, the product, both as the instruments and records must be absolutely uniform. It calls for specialists to distribute the product-those who, by musical training and equipment or facilities are competent to offer the public an artistic product in an intelligent manner. (Hearings III at 488-9)

> I claim we represent a specialty product and that it requires an organization of specialists for distribution. The employees must be educated and trained. ... There is no question in my mind as to the necessity of marketing a product, such as the Victor, as well as many others, under a uniform system, the most important part of which provides for uniform prices. (Hearings III at 492)

Representatives of the automobile industry also spoke at the hearings. Henry E. Bodman

of Packard Motors explained both the services that Packard required from its dealers and how it

arranged for those dealers to be reimbursed for such services:

> Now take the service principles... of the Packard Company... They require of the dealer that he have a location in a convenient and in a conspicuous place in the city; They require him to have a repair shop of certain dimensions; they require him to have a force of a certain size, and a certain number of these men must be factory-trained, expert men. The size of this repair [shop] must bear a relation to the number of cars in use in the territory. There must be given to the purchaser what is known as free service, which means that for the first thirty days all adjustments that car may need shall be given free ...(FTC at 670-71)

> It is absolutely essential ... that this service should be kept up, that its excellence should be maintained, and that the goodwill that goes with the car should be protected. Experience has shown ... that they [dealers] cannot insure the excellence of this service without allowing to the dealer and seeing that he gets a margin which ... is 20 percent above the wholesale price (FTC at 673) .[29]

---

[29] Bodman also explains (FTC at 672) that Packard rebated to the customer all the profits Packard made on the resale of used cars, avoiding the enforcement problem discussed by Klein and Murphy (1988 at 293) of how used car "trade-ins" can be employed to circumvent RPM.

As discussed in Section III-B, the Ford Motor Company also used RPM. Ford's representative, Alfred Lucking, told a similar story of how Ford used RPM to induce provision of a number of services, including having dealers teach their customers how to drive (Hearings I at 222):

> The Ford Company recognized early the fact that in order to build up a successful business it would be necessary to establish a system in which each purchaser or user of a Ford automobile should receive prompt and loyal service; that is, his car should be kept in good condition, in order that he might have first-class service and uninterrupted service. The relation between the Ford Motor Co. and its product is not completed when it has received the price paid by the dealer. This relation continues on during the entire life of the machine sold, and the success of that machine is regarded as of vital consequence to the company.
>
> The company's business has been built up to its present proportions by maintaining an organization consisting of dealers in every part of the country - I think about 6,000 - who were under contract obligations not only to maintain a garage and a stock of parts for quick repairs, but also to show purchasers how to use and handle and conserve the car, instructing them how to run it, and following and watching every car, remedying the defects, and making it please and satisfy the customer. None of these things is done by the cut-price cutthroat, who has no interest in the car or the business. When by his tricky practices he succeeds in taking customers away from their regular dealer the Ford Co. loses its best dealers and salesmen, and the company loses its reputation. The purchasers have troubles with the car that could easily and simply be corrected by any person having knowledge, but there is no one in the vicinity to instruct them. Hence follow dissatisfied customers, loss of the best advertisers-satisfied customers-loss of reputation, loss of sales and loss of business.

Thus, the Telser (1960) special services efficiency rationale was stated clearly by the manufacturers of gramophones and automobiles. They needed RPM to insure dealers' services for their new products, services that took many forms for these complex goods.

It is not immediately clear why advertising would be an important rationale for the use of RPM on complex goods. With the exception of the book selling industry, however, the complicated goods that used RPM appear to have come onto the market after the first wave of RPM around 1880.

E. Vertical Free-Riding on Brand Names

Participants in the hearings also made presentations indicating that they used RPM to alleviate concerns with vertical externalities, along the lines of Klein and Murphy (1988). In particular, one recurrent theme was that retailers reduced the price on branded articles and used them as loss leaders. Such discounting would signal to customers that other bargains were available in their stores. According to Brandeis (Reports I at 14):

> The manufacturer creates by his efforts and expenditure of money a reputation;...They [the price-cutters] know that if people are brought into the store and if shredded wheat, which can be had at 2 cents below standard price, is up in the fourth floor they will sell besides other things. On the route through the store until the shredded wheat is reached are spread a series of baits of just the kind of things the woman who wants shredded wheat will probably be tempted to buy...

Samuel Bloomingdale of Bloomingdale's Department Store stated (quoted in FTC at 811-2) that "[t]he cutting of fixed prices is done for the purpose of luring purchasers into the store in the hope that other goods of a similar character may be obtained at cut prices." George J. Schulte, representing the St. Louis Retail Grocers' Association, the St. Louis Master Butchers' Association, and the Missouri Retail Merchants' Association (Hearings II at 182-3) stated "[Price cutters] do not cut the profit because the profit is too large, but rather to fool the public into believing that their store is the most economical at which to trade or because they want to foist their own brands, the value of which the consuming public does not know." Similarly, according to J. George Frederick of *Advertising/Selling Magazine* (FTC at 549):

> The fact of price maintenance may be defined to a large degree as purchasing advertising. I mean not purchasing, but stealing advertising from someone who has paid for it, and securing it at a very much lower rate of expenditure than that concern from whom it was stolen paid for it. In other words, ... an entire advertisement of an entire page, mainly composed of unbranded articles, is sweetened up or made lively, so to speak, by a single small insertion in the middle of the ad, advertising at a tremendously cut price, at a loss, some article which has a reputation, that in essence and almost by ... [here the carbon printing fades]

A submission from a piece by Charles Thaddeus Terry (unidentified, Hearings I at 131) made essentially the same point:

> When manufacturers 25 years ago began to determine that they would fix the resale price at which their goods were to be offered to the public for sale, ... [t]hey did this as a matter of self-preservation. ... They did it because they had advertised their goods, put large sums of money into the advertising, and made their brands valuable, and they felt as a matter of right to prevent another man from using these brands and the costly advertisement that went with them, not for the purpose of selling these brands, but for the purpose of selling other goods unbranded at a greater profit. Manufacturers became convinced that this was a method of stealing their advertising, as it undoubtedly was, and that it not only was stealing advertising, but destructive of their market.

As discussed above in Section II, while the desire to deter loss-leading has been a constant theme in the history of RPM, little economic analysis has been done on this phenomena. It may be possible, however, to place the concepts in these quotations in the framework of the current economic literature. Consistent with Klein and Murphy, by engaging in loss-leading, retailers were vertically free-riding on manufacturer's name brands. In the terms of the Klein-Murphy analysis, retailers were being overcompensated for manufacturers' promotional efforts. In terms of Klein and Leffler, retailers used loss leading to capture part of the signal (or performance bond) being generated by the national advertising. Indeed, Professor Lee Galloway of New York University (Hearings I at 76) described loss leading as "a pretty cute scheme devised by big department stores to get free advertising at the expense of the advertising of the nationally distributed product."[30] In the terms of Marvel and McCafferty (1985) analysis, loss-leading is likely to occur with established, branded products because these are the products for which vertical free-riding is more valuable for a new entrant store than an established retail firm. In effect, retailers engaged in vertical free-riding to obtain certification for their own enterprises by associating themselves with well-known brands, the reverse of the earlier Marvel-McCafferty (1984) story, which posits that manufacturers look to retailers for certification. Thus, when a

---

[30] Nowhere in the hearings did I come across the modern economic term "free-riding". Frederick and Terry, however, used the term "stealing", which, while perhaps not technically correct, conveys the same essential meaning.

leading brand engaged in national advertising, it may have been acting to advertise (and certify) all those retailers who were using that brand as a loss leader.

From the presentations in the hearing, however, it is not clear why known brands would object to being used to certify retailers. Nor does the current economic theory speak directly to this question. It may be, however, that primarily low-quality retailers used loss-leading on known brands to certify themselves. If so, the poor view customers gained of such retailers may have rubbed off on the brands used as loss leaders.[31] In terms of Klein and Leffler (1980), loss leading may permit low-quality retailers to take away from producers and capture for themselves part of the performance bond attached to high-quality branded products.

Supporters of RPM also directly spoke on concepts similar to Springer and Frech's (1986) theory that RPM was needed to deter fraud. Indeed, the 1916 and 1917 versions of the Stephens bill was entitled "To Protect the Public Against Dishonest Advertising and False Pretenses in Merchandising." Charles Dushkind, counsel for the Tobacco Merchant's Association, argued (Hearings II at 112):

> ... [L]et us consider the consumer, who is apparently the only gainer by price-cutting. While the jobbers and dealers are busily engaged in trade war, and in their efforts to throw one another out of business, the consumer is getting the benefit. He buys his goods so much cheaper, and why should any legislation be passed that will make the wealthy merchant still wealthier at the expense of the customer? But this question can readily be answered. The consumer is not benefited by price cutting on standard and trade-marked goods. On the contrary, the standard goods are commonly used as a means to defraud the consumer. The standard goods are invariably employed to advertise fake sales and fraudulent bargain counters to attract the consumer's attention and to thus lure him into a store where after he purchases the advertised standard article at a loss of a few cents, they always succeed in selling him some unknown article at an exorbitant price.

Similarly, according to George L. Record (FTC at 1256-7, representing both the Ingersoll Watch company and the Fair Trade League, but apparently speaking for the B.V.D. underwear company):

---

[31] This concept appears to have been only briefly mentioned in the economic literature. See, for example, Steiner (1985 at 161), Klein and Murphy (1988 at 293) and Gerstner and Hess (1991 at 873.) For a discussion of this issue in the marketing literature, see Jacoby and Mazursky (1984).

[P]rice cutting breeds substitution, and deception. We use every honorable effort to sustain our brand and to prevent anyone from using it improperly, and my opinion is that if our prices to retailers had not been cut, some of the substitution would never have taken place, as a fair price and a fair profit to the seller removes the temptation to be deceptive.

Congressman Stephens (Hearings III at 430) compared the effects of his bill to that of a consumer protection statute of the same era:

> The pure-food law [of 1906] compelled the producer to sell goods which were not deleterious, and next it made him brand exactly what they were and not sell fraudulent substitutes, and next it compels him to state exactly how much his package contains. You see, he is compelled to tell the truth within certain limits. This is accomplished by a prohibition against certain wrongful acts. This bill seeks to obtain the same general result but by the opposite method. Instead of prohibitions against evils, it allows a course of dealing which will encourage the good dealing and thus eliminate the evils. ... This bill would take away the opportunity to use standard goods, which the people know about as of a certain price and value, from being used as a bait and lure for the sale of unknown goods, because the public would be led to think that the unknown goods were being sold at the same relative value as the standard goods, when the latter are sold at cut prices.

Thus, proponents of RPM argued that it was needed to deter "bait and switch" tactics, similar to what Springer and Frech (1986) describe. While retailers used manufacturers' brand names to draw customers into their stores, manufacturers received no income from this practice, as their goods were not the ones being sold. Thus, RPM prevented dealers from being overcompensated for promotional services by manufacturers, as Klein and Murphy hypothesized. In effect, as the Klein-Leffler theory implies, RPM was needed to keep retailers honest.

V. Conclusion

The numerous efficiency explanations for RPM generated by modern economists are not new. Indeed, all of the prominent theories are replicated in various forms by early advocates of RPM, acting almost entirely without the help of economists. In particular, some of the economic discussions of the efficiency aspects of branding are quite elegant, anticipating the relevant economic literature by almost 70 years. While today's economic theories may appear to be "pie in the sky" to their critics, they were certainly real enough to businessmen over 70 years ago.

An examination of the hearings reveal that RPM was used to protect investments in shelf space and product promotions at the retail level, promotions which may have been complements of national advertising. These conclusions also explain why there were no RPM cases prior to 1885 and why participants in the hearings believed that national advertising was the catalyst for RPM. The famous Telser (1960) story of free-riding on special services fits well with the examples of gramophones and automobiles. Hearing participants also expressed concern that price-cutting and "loss-leading" led to vertical free-riding on brands and reputation in order to capture manufacturer's performance bonds or generate certification of retailers, which may represent a combination of the efficiency rationales described by Klein and Murphy (1988) and Marvel and McCafferty (1985). They also argued that RPM was used to alleviate consumer deception, along the lines of Springer and Frech (1986).

A review of the hearings generates two other insights. First, the hearings reveal that the current economic literature has failed to properly address the interrelationship between loss leading and RPM. Second, the rise of RPM in the 1880s can be directly attributed to the rise in importance of advertised branded goods. Given this, and the fact that horizontal restraints predate RPM by at least several centuries, it seems unlikely that the primary motivation for RPM is cartel facilitation.

Bibliography

Adams, Walter, and Brock, James W., "The Political Economy of Industry Exemptions," Washburn Law Review 29 (1990) 215-237.

Blecher, Maxwell M., "The Impact of GTE-Sylvania on Antitrust Jurisprudence," Antitrust Law Journal, 60 (1991) 17-27.

Bittlingmayer, George, "Resale Price Maintenance in the Book Trade with an Application to Germany," Journal of Institutional and Theoretical Economics 144 (1988) 789-812.

Bowman, Ward S. Jr., "The Prerequisites and Effects of Retail Price Maintenance," University of Chicago Law Review 22 (1955) 825-873.

Breit, William, "Resale Price Maintenance: What Do Economists Know and When Did They Know It," Journal of Institutional and Theoretical Economics 147 (1991) 72-90.

Cherington, Paul T., Advertising as a Business Force, Arno (1976, first published in 1913) New York.

Comanor, William B., "Vertical Price-Fixing, Vertical Market Restrictions, and the New Antitrust Policy," Harvard Law Review 98 (1985) 983-1002.

Easterbrook, Frank H., "The Limits of Antitrust," Texas Law Review 63 (1984) 1-40.

Federal Trade Commission, "Conference on Resale Price Maintenance," Volumes 1 through 7 (1917) Washington, D.C. (FTC)

Gelhorn, Ernest, Antitrust Law and Economics, West Publishing Co. (1976) St. Paul, MN.

Gerstner, Eitan, and Hess, James D., "A Theory of Channel Price Promotions," American Economic Review 81 (1991) 872-886.

Goldberg, Victor, "The Free Rider Problem, Imperfect Pricing, and the Economics of Retail Servicing," Northwestern University Law Review 79 (1984) 736-757.

Hellman, Elizabeth, "Vertical Territorial and Customer Restrictions in the Franchising Industry," Columbia Journal of Law and Social Problems 10 (1974) 497-523.

Ippolito, Pauline M., Resale Price Maintenance: Economic Evidence From Litigation, Federal Trade Commission (1988) Washington, D.C.

Ippolito, Pauline M., "Resale Price Maintenance: Economic Evidence From Litigation," Journal of Law and Economics 34 (1991) 263-294.

Jacoby, Jacob, and Mazursky, David, "Linking Brand and Retailer Images: Do the Potential Risks Outweigh the Potential Benefits," Journal of Retailing 60 (1984) 105-22.

Kelly, Kenneth, "The Role of the Free Rider in Resale Price Maintenance: The Loch Ness Monster of Antitrust Captured," George Mason Law Review 10 (1988).

Klein, Benjamin, and Leffler, Keith, "The Role of Market Forces in Assuring Contractual Performance," Journal of Political Economy 89:4 (1981) 615-42.

Klein, Benjamin, and Murphy, Kevin M., "Vertical Restraints as Contract Enforcement Mechanisms," Journal of Law and Economics 31 (1988) 265-298.

Lynch, Michael, "The `Steiner Effect': A Prediction from a Monopolistically Competitive Model Inconsistent with any Combination of Pure Monopoly or Competition," Federal Trade Commission Working Paper #141, August 1986.

Marvel, Howard P., and McCafferty, Stephen, "Resale Price Maintenance and Quality Certification," Rand Journal of Economics 15 (1984) 346-59.

Marvel, Howard P., and McCafferty, Stephen, "The Welfare Effects of Resale Price Maintenance," Journal of Law and Economics 28 (May 1985) 363-379.

McCraw, Thomas K., Prophets of Regulation, Harvard University Press (1984) Boston.

Ornstein, Stanley I., "Resale Price Maintenance and Cartels," Antitrust Bulletin 30 (1985) 401-432.

Peppin, John C., "Price-Fixing Agreements Under the Sherman Anti-Trust Law," California Law Review 28 (1940) 297.

Posner, Richard, Antitrust: Cases, Economic Notes, and Other Materials, West Publishing Co. (1974), St. Paul, MN.

Restrictive Trade Practises Commission (Canada), Report On An Inquiry Into Loss-Leader Selling, Queen's Printer and Controller of Stationery (1955), Ottawa.

Rosch, J. Thomas, "The State of Antitrust Law," Antitrust Law Journal, 60 (1991) 3-9.

Scherer, F.M. and Ross, David, Industrial Market Structure and Economics Performance, Houghlin Mifflin Company, Boston (3rd edition, 1989)

Seligman, Edwin R.A., and Love, Robert A., Price Cutting and Price Maintenance, Harper & Brothers (1932) New York.

Springer, Robert F., and Frech, H. E., III, "Deterring Fraud: The Role of Resale Price Maintenance," Journal of Business 59:3 (1986) 433-449.

Steiner, Robert L., "The Nature of Vertical Restraints," Antitrust Bulletin 30 (1985) 143-198.

Telser, Lester G., "Why Should Manufacturers Want Fair Trade?", Journal of Law and Economics 3 (1960) 86-105.

Taussig, F.W., "Price Maintenance," American Economic Review 4 (Supplement, 1916) 170-184.

Tosdale, H.R., "Price Maintenance," American Economic Review 8 (March 1918) 28-47.

U.S. House of Representatives, Committee on Interstate and Foreign Commerce, 63rd Congress, "Hearings on H.R. 13305, a Bill to Prevent Discrimination in Price and to Provide for Publicity of Prices to Dealers and the Public," (1915). (Hearings I.)

U.S. House of Representatives, Committee on Interstate and Foreign Commerce, 64th Congress, "Hearings on H.R. 13568, a Bill to Protect the Public Against Dishonest Advertising and False Pretenses in Merchandising," (1916). (Hearings II.)

U.S. House of Representatives, Committee on Interstate and Foreign Commerce, 64th Congress, "Hearings on H.R. 13568, a Bill to Protect the Public Against Dishonest Advertising and False Pretenses in Merchandising," (1917). (Hearings III.)

U.S. House of Representatives, Committee on Energy and Commerce, Subcommittee on Commerce, Transportation, and Tourism, "Oversight of FTC Law Enforcement," Serial No. 98-123 (1984).

U.S. Senate, Committee on the Judiciary, "Hearing on a Bill to Amend the Sherman Act Regarding Retail Competition," (S. 865) Serial No. J-101-10 (1989).

White, Lawrence J., "Resale Price Maintenance and the Problem of Marginal and Intramarginal Customers," Contemporary Policy Issues 3 (1985) 17-21.

www.ingramcontent.com/pod-product-compliance
Lightning Source LLC
Chambersburg PA
CBHW081313180526
45170CB00007B/2690